# Midas Touch

## Mike Horwood

Published by Ward Wood Publishing
6 The Drive
Golders Green
London NW11 9SR
www.wardwoodpublishing.co.uk

The right of Mike Horwood to be identified as author of this work has been asserted by him in accordance with the Copyright, Designs and Patent Act, 1988.

Copyright © 2010 Mike Horwood
ISBN: 978-0-9566602-2-0
British Library Cataloguing in Publication Data. A CIP record for this book can be obtained from the British Library.

Designed and typeset in Palatino Linotype
by Ward Wood Publishing.
Cover design by Mike Fortune-Wood.
Printed and bound in Great Britain by
MPG Biddles Ltd, King's Lynn, Norfolk.

# Contents

## Prologue: Two Poems From Finland

## Midas Touch

# Prologue: Two Poems From Finland

## 1. *Winter Swans*

In Finland today, the morning
mist has gone that collected
under the sodden birch trees.
The weather's been warm enough
to melt much of the snow

but the last piles still raise
white backs behind the hedge,
like swans drifting south,
while a line of packed-ice footprints
crosses newly exposed grass.

I've partially closed my living
room blinds so the sun won't fade
the painting of forest mushrooms,
picked, cleaned and spread
on a chopping board ready for dinner.

Still life. It's too early to cook,
so I stand at the window, steam
rising from coffee. When I sit,
the chair feels warm, as if someone
had left it only moments before.

## 2. *Family*

Doorstep, garden
path, a bush, smell
of grass after rain,

the soft *pip* of water
falling onto leaves,

halo round the light
on the garage wall.

And there's
the mother hare
between two offspring,

six ears silhouetted
against the lamp-
lit tarmac.

# Midas Touch

# Midas Touch

I was about to take the first bite
from an apple when it happened.
My teeth skidded over the surface,
dragging lip from gum.
I dropped the thing like I'd been scalded
and it smashed. Glass, not gold.

I reached out to a chair, paused,
then laid my hand on. In ripples,
starting at my fingertips, the wood
paled down the back, across the seat,
down the legs. Paled to transparency.
Nobody'd sit there again.

The strangest part was looking
into a mirror and seeing
right through myself, all the way
back to childhood, like a story
I'd thought left behind in the dark.
This touch was its sequel.

# Magnifying Glass

At school we've all looked into one,
hovered it over a blade of grass
and seen the green sword's cutting edge.

We've peered at the tips of our fingers,
the geography of whorls writ suddenly large,
and followed the Nile across green and yellow
to Abri, El Khandaq, Khartoum.

When the boy at the back raised his to one eye
and winked hugely, we laughed,
but the side of his face

                        stepped out of itself.

At arm's length it made trees shrink
and stand on their heads,
a single leg pointing up
into a grassy sky.

# Matinée

We'd arrive before the doors opened
and queue beside a stained brick wall.
I looked at the line in front,
afraid we'd not get in, but once

through the doors it was a new world.
Thick crimson carpet cushioned
footsteps, muffled noise.
My gilt face looked from the rail.
We climbed the wide stairs.

It was a world with its own language –
*foyer, intermission, Wall's hot dog, Kia-ora* –
words only heard at the cinema:
even *curtain* meant something different here.

A place where children climbed out
through bedroom windows and sat
on the roof, beneath stars.

*Exit* meant leaving the story
behind in the dark,
*what happened next,* lost for ever.

Borne by the flow into
the shock of light;
shopfronts, bus stop, cracks
in paving all oddly luminous,
some of their reality syphoned off
into the film. Some of *its* fantasy
seeping out into my world.

# Nature Study, 1962

Miss Smith taught us about stamens
with anthers that made pollen.
The pollen stuck to the legs of bees
who rubbed it off on the stigma.
We drew it in our books.

Next we did trees. Miss Smith had
light brown hair and a chart that showed
the shapes of oak, willow, elm.
She propped it up against the blackboard
and we drew the outlines in our books.

We were allowed to leave our desks
without putting our hands up to check
the shapes more closely, and the names,
but never more than two at the front
at one time. Wind carried the trees' pollen.

Miss Smith had shoes that clicked
when she crossed the room and a hard smack.
`Now we will go to look at the poplars
that grow along the road beside the school,'
she said. We stood in pairs, holding hands

and followed her out of the classroom.
Poplars were the tallest and straightest
trees on the chart. Miss Smith walked
with funny, short, quick steps because
her skirt was too tight at the knees.

We stood in a line and looked at the poplars
and cars. Miss Smith said, `This wind
must be blowing the pollen about.'
A police car stopped and two policemen
offered to help us across the road.

`We don't want to cross,´ Miss Smith told them.
`We´re looking at the poplars.´ The policemen
were tall. They stood very straight beside
Miss Smith and looked at the poplars, too.
We all looked for a very long time.

# Windows

My father was a glazier. Staring
into the green, subaqueous light

of panes stacked in his storeroom, my face
looked back, pressed between surfaces.

The sash window of my first bedsit
was jammed. I sweated in that airless space,

but when I took up astronomy the frosty draught
from the attic skylight was my companion

as I viewed the heavenly bodies
with my eye against the lens.

# Wanting Out

In the dusk I'd wrap curtains round me
and turn. Striped linen twisted
above my head and gripped. A cocoon.

I was in the window, but hidden -
the genie in the magic lamp -
wishes granted if you'd let me out.

# Our Favourite Game

Playing at hide-and-seek
I found the greatest freedom
in your slow count to a hundred.
When I heard footsteps approaching

I screwed my eyes shut, curled in a ball,
held my breath till I saw orange.
But we quickly moved beyond seeker
and hidden, adapted the rules.

In the orchard we acted out
sinner and saint. The smell
of a trodden on, rotten apple
still brings it all back – sickly, but sweet.

By the railway embankment, caution
was called for in the exposed space
beside the track. The hum of a nearing train,
its drone when receding, signalled

a change to the roles of mourner
and lately departed. We played
the living seeking the dead.
Or as sleeper you hid, insomniac

I faltered through dawn's sleepless doubts
to the greatest refinement of all,
when I, as seeker, hid what I sought
and you delved into that secret.

# Musical Chairs

At first, he didn't realise
how musical his chairs were.
They had obscure talents
and were in secret communication
with desirable elements
in his environment.

One morning in July, the air
pulsed with excitement
as he warmed himself, and the chairs
beat time with a rhythm as fluent
as a message in code.

A little bird sang the accompaniment.
The tree swayed, the mat was astonished
and the walls felt betrayed.

For him, it was all a game:
the struggle to reach a seat,
victory meant being left alone.

# Nervous

It was nothing like flipping
the light switch – more like
his palm on a hotplate
then turning it on. It began

with noticing how the chairs looked at him.
When he thought himself alone
a thousand eyes watched
as he moved about his home.

He listened. The walls maintained
their silence but the bedcover
practised temptation.
`Lie with me,´ it whispered.

Doors and tables adopted
an inquisitorial tone
but at the critical moment
he chose to ignore them.

It had been his constant plan
to deny these odd appearances.
He didn't wish to be caught
engaged in conversation with the furniture.

# First Night

This is my finest hour, on the stage
receiving well-deserved applause.
What a show! I'm bending forward,
muscles tensed, head bowed, basking.
This feels like sunlight shining on me,
warming me right through.

I raise my head and torso.
The audience is a blur, a mass
of sound, claps that fill the air
so I bow again, tingling, rosy.

And tonight there *will* be roses. I smell
their scent already. Champagne corks will pop,
the spume frothing, me looking over my shoulder
like an actor looking into the wings.

# Clairvoyance

It was like learning to read
all over again. The most ordinary
words, like *spam* and *bank*,
were pregnant with new meaning.

Clairvoyance must be something like this,
she thought, stepping into the house
and hearing sounds that had died
some hours before.

The chairs stated their position with force,
offering a seat in clarification;
the curtains held a rush of air
in their folds that murmured to her.

As a child she had dreamed
of a mirror that recorded on its surface
every image it had ever reflected
and the power that would give over things.

# Things

There are these things:
one half of a double door stands ajar,

through the frosted pane of its closed partner
the curtain's blue stain visible on the wall.

The empty floor echoes to no footfall.
A mirror reflects a key on the hallstand.

These things are troubled -
they know exactly what's happened.

# Dining Out

was not an occasion most likely to suggest
the serving up of home truths.

Nor was his *cock in wine*
an encouraging start
to translating the complexities
of that evening's menu.

There's no denying he was hooked
on sloe eyes and the special creaminess
of a dark-haired woman's skin,

yet he never felt a thing
as she worked her blade
the length of a sole
and separated flesh from bone.

He lowered his eyes, though,
when she told tales from her schooldays,
and her account of the boy
she'd sat next to in class
was flavoured with spices he could not name.

# Witness

There are days when nature
knows more than she tells,
when shoots heave aside loam to reach light
and that stillness under waving branches
betrays intense concentration.
Each knobble and groove of the tree's bark
tells the tale of seeds' dispersal
and the trunk, rigid with excitement, reflects on it.

A flicker in the bracken stops him dead,
afraid to move a foot
that might disturb the murmuring grass.
Leaves reveal the wind's contours,
while in his focused eye is mirrored
all this watching, listening world.

# Deliberately Getting Out At Cricket

She had a passion for the game
and on dates she'd take me to matches,
but she had to explain the rules
and still I didn't understand.

`Cricket's as varied as life,' she said.
`It's as complex,' I replied.

In the school where she taught
there were fixtures on Wednesdays.
The boys laughed
and played dares in the pauses -

`If you don't get out this over,
you love Miss Mitchell.' Grey-haired,
tweed-skirted. Maths.

The batsman's dismissal minutes later
was blatant cricket suicide.
An enquiry was held next day,
the air in the head's study
electric with tension.

She seemed to take the matter seriously.
`It has to do with trust,' she told me.
`That player betrayed his team mates.'

She watched closely, as if waiting
for me to play a stroke.

I only said, `How bizarre',
and received a look that accused me
of deliberately getting out at cricket.

# Verruca´s End

When the postman dropped
the decree nisi onto the mat
with a light slap
I was in the bathroom, soaking
my foot. The ring of dead,
yellowed skin had softened
and swollen with water.

I pulled and it spiralled loose,
one end attached
to the ghostly white maggot
that buried its head
in the red crater.

A tug began to dislodge it,
the last hooks anchored to tissue,
till it finally parted
and blood welled where the root
had been dragged from flesh.

# Cleansed

These things always reminded him:
cold water hitting the flat bottom of an enamel sink,

the feel of a bar of soap embedded with grit,
the trickle of water conducted along an open gutter

in a bare concrete floor.
These things never failed to remind him of this:

the disinfectant smell of that bar of soap,
and of how he had washed his hands of all that.

# Sun Going Down

The bark of the silver birch
reflects sunlight like a mirror;
I'm looking through the masts
of a fleet of ships made of glass.

And later a pink glow
flushes the tops of the pines
like the mating colouration
of an endangered species.

# Marsyas

He had to be flayed
for the crime of playing on his pipe.
So his wrists were bound together,
he was drawn up and suspended
from a limb of the closest tree,
while the tree tried to see through her leaves
what was happening.

`Please don't do it. Don't tear me
away from myself,' he begged.

But the skin was dragged off his back
and loins, exposing muscle fibres
to stinging air. His nipples were peeled
from his breast and the network
of pulsating veins and entrails revealed.
Ripped testicles bled their seed
down his thighs.

When she understood what had been done to him
the tree mingled her tears with the blood
that dripped to the earth
beneath his limp, drained body.

# Cyparissus

With his spear he wounded
the one he loved most,
and brought at last to bay by grief,
he asked the god of poetry
to let him mourn her loss forever.

Attracted to Rhodope's slopes,
he heard one who'd lost his wife
by an error of judgement
sing of the love of the gods
and lawless passion.

# These Words

These words are wearing
their Sunday best.
They do not slouch
with hands in pockets
but stand up straight
in regimented lines,
according to custom.
And when they walk
they plant their feet
firmly on the ground
and step with honest tread.

These are not the words
that stay out all night,
get lost on the wrong
side of town, so drunk
they don't remember their names
or where they've come from.
Words that are never there
when you need them.

These words are not mine;
they're for common usage,
their look conventional.
On their best behaviour,
do they seem too formal?

These words,
in their Sunday best,
like guests at a wedding
with gifts to present,
sit with their meanings
folded in their laps.

# Clearing Out The Attic

You know the way it goes. The usual
start. A wet Sunday. You've been meaning
to do this for months. Meaning years.
At last, you get the ladder out.

Poking your head up through the trap
reminds you of peering into the ribs
of an old wooden ship. It's time
you lightened its cargo of relics.

So you crouch in the dust and half-light,
fingering through a box of vinyl
L.P.s, humming to the rafters, telling
Angie, *You could say we're satis...*

But your song stops dead when a key
drops from one of the covers. The key to your last
home. The one you couldn't find when you moved
and had to change the lock for its new owner.

# Little Arrows

I'd pictured a length, sectioned
like cane, and flexible,
but this is smooth and rigid
and much smaller than I expected.

The flight feathers have been trimmed
with a razor, leaving them stiff,
like razors themselves
to cut through the air.

The arrowhead's no more
than a metal point,
not proud of the shaft, but flush –
for ease of extraction?

I imagine it penetrating
my back, sinking a well-hole
between the shoulders, missing
the lungs and piercing my heart.

I run a finger from tip
to tail, roll it, then press up
with my thumbs but there's no give.
Then before my eyes

it begins to fade and grow lighter.
If matter burned with no flame
or heat, it would disappear
like this. I'm left empty-handed

so I struggle to my feet
and limp across the room
to the crunching sound
of some gritty residue on the floor.

# Underwater

Low tide, the foreshore
revealed in sunlight.
Earlier I'd waded there,
too near the dark mass
of submerged rocks, lacy spume
that bubbled round their tips,
uncertain what my feet
would find under their next step,
unsettled by a swell that pushed
insistent as desire.

That night I dreamt an eye,
high above the waves' deep throb.
Under the blanket I sniffed
the salt and secret smell of the sea.

Years later, weightless in the clear
water of the sunny Aegean,
I looked through perspex
at beckoning weeds,
light rippling over sand,
watched by silent, knowing fish.

# It Happened Like This....

Midas, returning through the wood,
eager to test this new power
he still doesn't dare to believe in.

Oak leaves turn to gold.
                          His mouth dries.

Conviction strengthens as he picks up a stone,
brushes his hand over blades of grass, strokes
a feather with the tip of his finger.
                          All's gold.


A crease comes and goes on his brow
when the apple he plucks is useless for eating;
at first not daring to think
                          the gift
of touch has gone for good.

Broken bread drops crumbs of gold and his joy
cracks
          under the pressure of what this means.

He looks back to the wood he's just left
where sunlight paints the leaves gold.

# The Pursuit Of Signs

These things he knew: the wind's bite
on his face coming over the frozen lake,

the scuffed impression of spread wings in snow
where tiny footprints terminated.

Elsewhere would be tufts of fur, the ruin of a skull
bleached salt white, brittle as ice.

He knew the curve of its eye socket and jaw,
like the signs on a shaman's fetish.

# A Line Drawn On The Air

My garden is in shade
but along the riverbank,
trees are bright
with yellow light.
I see the sunshine move
over the water, across the lawn
to the plum tree, a line
drawn on the air.

All summer we watched the plums,
pale green pips that slowly
swelled. The faint crease
in their skin turned to a rift
and began to blush
on the side that faced the sun.

They're ready to eat now,
though I failed to place
the moment they changed
from unripe to ripe.

And you? Do you notice
such things? The border
between green grass and parched?
Or the moment you crossed
the watershed into a new
catchment area, suddenly
part of a new river?

# Apple

There we were among the apple trees,
me up in the branches, dropping
fruit to you on the ground.
Green and scarcely ripe

we carried our bagful home,
then warmed our faces in the oven's heat
as juices bubbled
through crumble and browned.

And so it comes round again,
the season between tart and sweet.
Branches, loaded with clusters,
sway as slowly in this wind
as the limb I clung on to when I stretched out
to add to our haul.

# Bream

That day,
      like a Chinese watercolour,
grey trees in a pale mist,
      mist and shapes
merge in the distance,
two figures beside a lake.

A silent day with blank spaces,

comfortless as going barefoot on the stony shore.
And what seems like stillness at first glance

is slight and intermittent stirring
among the dripping boughs,

like the suspicion of movement underwater
at the point where vision and imagination meet.

Water fills the eyes that stare into the gloom.

Beneath the glint of surface light,
shadows waver
      like dark brushstrokes.

A blink,
      and there it is
a large bream
has moved out of the depths.

It drifts among the stems,
sifts the silt from generations
of water plants, sucks
and blows yellow ochre clouds
and leaves these signs behind:

pockmarks in the mud, lines
where its tail has dragged.

# A Seagull

A broken wave slides suds
over glinting sand. Lodged between grains
last bubbles spangle and burst.

Two gulls struggle with the wind;
dip, bank and rise. One's torn off and flung,
as if from a sling, into the haze.

I've seen this, or something so like it
so many times, I impose memory
on the new, as if it's mine already.

I saw a time-lapse film once
where wisps of cloud above a windy valley
swirled and vanished like that sea foam.

I remember that single gull, too,
padding the shoreline, the feathers along
its back and neck lifted and tugged at.

# Those Days

I could imagine the days
                    were tiles
on a floor
                    I walked over.
A chequered floor
                    where `one thing
led to another'
                    with the sense
of inevitability
                    that black
following white
                    following black
lends to a sequence.

Or think of the days as the bed of a river that glides
smoothly on with the confidence a river has in the bed's
always being there.

Maybe the air trembled with a peal
of thunder, far off, below the horizon,
as the river slid, unquestioning
as glass, over the lip, hung

for a second, wonderstruck
at the floor's
                    not being there,
                    then fell,
                    breaking
                    apart,
                    the thunder rushing up to meet it.

I could say that I live
in a house by a river,
with tiled floors,
mountains in the distance.

# Crossing The Alps

Two hours out of the village
I'd climbed the mountain's shaded side
two months deeper into winter.

Coarse grass was brown, ground water
had flowed over the path
and frozen. I stopped.

The smooth sheet sloped down,
curled round the overhang, drips
falling onto rocks in the gully.

I put one foot on the ice,
shifted my weight, hesitated,
then moved my other foot forward.

Five steps carried me over, my pulse racing.
I stood on the brink, dislodging pebbles
and knew I had no way back.

As I climbed higher, peaks
reared up behind the black
ridgeback. Cresting it,

I toppled into the new view. Bank
behind bank of ice anchored on stone
all the way to Italy.

The village I'd left,
tethered to the foothills
by a winding cord of tarmac.

# Sunday

Usually we go shopping
at the hypermarket on the edge of town
where the totem-pole of household names
rises higher than a church spire.

First Ted takes the car
to the automatic wash.
I've got the kids cleaned
and dressed by the time he's back.

On the road we watch the skyline
till one sings out the ritual chant,
`I saw the shop tower first.'
Then we time how long it takes

to find a space among the rows
of many colours spread across the tarmac.
There's ice-cream all round
if we park beside a Jag.

Families file in and congregate
at game machines or Pizza Hut
while the music system plugs
the gaps in human noise.

The kids push a trolley each
along the beckoning aisles.
`Into the valley of temptation,'
says Ted, and grins and winks.

Our routine never alters.
At the bakery counter
Ted says, `Forgive us our daily bread.'
Every week the kids laugh

while I linger in the salty smell
of the cheese counter. Five years old again.
Women in their yellow tunics,
seamed stockings, smell of sour milk.

And *I*, or something dear to me, is lost.

# Flight Path

Birdsong pulls me up through dreams
two or three times.
Sunlit curtains billow. Then are still.

Through the open window
I hear a plane and doze.
It's 1962. Northolt. I'm swinging

from a peg in the cloakroom
of my first school, imagining
how I might hoist a foe to leave him

hanging, helpless, as the Romans did.
6,000 along the Appian Way,
nailed or tied to the woodwork.

School coats hang like ghosts
on hooks. Next, I'm in a museum hall
where the screech of birds is taped.

Pools of light puddle the dimness,
a hill and scaffold scene silhouetted
on a wall bathed in blue twilight.

Black wings stretch above pinioned limbs,
feathers sharp against the cheek
as a bird spears an eyeball. The tape plays.

....            ....            ....

8.15. I make coffee. Thrushes stalk the lawn.
Feeding their young, they're as single-minded
as a sniper. A worm twists

44

in a thrush's beak before slipping
down the greased darkness of a gullet.
And I'm trying to run away from this:

birds, Romans, twilight, dim blue light.
Something moves in the air, something
moves across the lawn, while I'm just thinking.

# From Now On

when I watch a mother bird cock her head,
using her body like a spear,
dart her beak at the ground,
and her chick rushes to her side
with urgent, open bill
and I register with what haste she pushes
the worm or grub at the grasping, pink gullet,

I will always see you,
kneeling on the floor in the middle
of that party, a dish
in your left hand, a fork in your right,
breaking lumps from a rich chocolate cake
and passing them into the open mouth
of a four-year-old girl.
I will remember the absorption of each,
intent on feeding and being fed
and a sweet brown ring around lips.

# My Finest Moment

Not the America of my first lie,
the Indian riches of the new world it opened,

nor the thought I could gloss
events as I wished, diverted

by imaginary rubies and gold.
Not nailing the lie to my mast

then mismanaging the purchase and sale of home
after home and living in debt for years.

Not dreaming your face on entering a party
then searching the rooms in vain,

but recognising the stillness
under waving branches,

due to a space
with the same shape as you.

# Gift

These things can look after themselves;
midsummer apples hang small and hard,
or lie in dew-soaked grass
in the shade below the trunks.

I look far beyond them,
where a night-dark sea rises
and falls with compelling rhythm,
the same that under-

scores Brahms' Fourth Symphony.
*Er lebte wie ein richtiger Künstler,*
you told me once. I see you too,
the sky as black as your hair.

The blind casts moonlight stripes
across my back in the same way
that the wind carries night scents.
These things need me to look after them.

You move under a palm. Your silhouette
crosses the moon-path on the water.
I bring you this vivid bloom,
this gift of luscious fruit with a waxy rind.

# Before The Fall

It's amazing how fast these leaves sink
through the air, like stones in water
or coins in a well
that swing from side to side
in short, quick arcs,
dancing their indecision.

Autumns, I dream of going back to my roots,
buried, like a tree's, in the dirt, twisted
in their unspeakable underworld.
I imagine exposing them, peeling back
bark to reveal the surprising
purity of their whiteness. Roots
that might have carried sap to green
leaves in the world before the fall.

# Trees Of My Youth

*These trees are possible, but*
*they have the look of trees*
*that have been deceived.*

Trees of my youth, with slender
anaemic trunks, stand in shade
at the end of my garden,
like ghosts competing for light.

In dreams they hear the sound
of hammering in a world
of tables and chairs, and frames
that hold paintings or glass.

Autumn is the hardest season.
The smell of smoke in the evening
air disturbs them. They comfort
each other, lock their arms together.

For a tree that has found its own way
to enjoy the sun and rain
each leaf it drops in autumn
hints at what might have been.

Bare branches etch the whole tale
on the sky. Through bare branches it's easy
to read weather signs, like looking,
through a frame, at a table or chair.

# Patience

They are there in the forest,
the witches, goblins, the heads
of grotesque devils and old men,

hiding in the tortured roots
of a wind-broken pine
or bog oak, in stunted limbs

of juniper and alder, twisted
by winter gales and snow
on exposed slopes.

It can take years of gazing
with empty eyes to feel the bend
and warp in the grain.

Then knives are sharpened, chisels
strike with a ring like metal on stone
and the wood releases its meaning.

# Wine, Women And Song

Like a difficult wine,
made from a sensitive grape,
summer here often fails.
But one year in ten
there are days when the air
is as soft and warm on the skin
as a lover's caress,
so unlike the burning sand
and dry thirst of southern lands.

Days that live in the memory
like the notes of a favourite melody
recalled through the years.

Memories with the clarity
of an amber Sauternes,
the essence of summer on the tongue
like the taste of the tongue
of a lover who left long ago.

# Grus Grus

*Kraa-kraa.*

First we hear them,
their call a repeated greeting
from beyond the treetops. Between

the highest branches we
glimpse dark shapes.
Then the first cranes appear in open sky

above the pines and birches,
towing their ragged V into view,
inscribing themselves on air.

The leading birds beat the wind,
the rear sail the slipstream,
drifting wide on its drag.

Head back till I'm giddy and
stumble, I watch their wake
spread across the surface of the sky.

The breeze lifts my hair
and I'm up there with them,
riding the tail of a kite.

As children we held hands in a line,
turned, and round the end child flew
on the force carried through our joined hands,

their feet almost leaving the ground.

# Busman's Holiday

The only illumination here
comes from the stained glass

lamp on my desk.
Its shade casts red

and gold on the walls.
And in the centre

of its glow there's a density,
like shadow, where

the maker's used a deeper
colour in the rose

motif's design, as if light
has thickened into matter.

That maker was my father,
the glazier, who worked

in stained glass
as a hobby. He

told me that the infinite
reflections in parallel

mirrors appear as
total darkness.

# Tiffany

My mother, a dressmaker,
                        often worked
with tiffany gauze.
                        I gathered the off-cuts,
loving the stuff's transparency.
                                It made
my world misty;
                        the same, but strange.

To show they'd died, I wrapped toy soldiers
in tiffany,
                        like mummies; still visible,
but removed
                        to their spirit world.

I best understood the story
of Jesus
                        making the blind man
                                            see
when I played a game of blindman's buff
with tiffany gauze
                        over my eyes.

# An Ordinary Day

It's early June and the morning sun
illuminates this page, my coffee cup,
a shiver of glass on my desk
and the hand that holds this pencil.

I'm looking down at the street
beyond my window, quiet in its
mid-morning Wednesday ordinariness,
exercising my words in this simple record.

You know the kind of thing I mean.
I want to evoke the nothing special of everyday
that makes it good to be alive.
I want to find the right phrase to show

the quality of sunlight
catching the leaves on the hedge and shrubs,
the way the wind pushes the scattered clouds.
When I lay my arm across the desk

in this patch of yellow light
it warms my skin without burning.
Through the open window I hear
the clatter and whirr

of a hand-pushed mower
a few gardens down the street.
In the pauses I can hear
the hum of traffic from the highway.

A woman and her dog pass
and stop to look at the parallel black lines
and gouged tarmac sliding off the road
into chipped slabs of paving

where yesterday a couple veered
under a lorry while tuning their radio.
I picked this shiver of glass from the side-walk,
its point far sharper than my pencil's.

# Domestic Geography

The vase stands on a polished table;
red roses lend to a cool room
an opulence and elegance.
Dark wood shines like water
where it catches light.

In Alpine white the four walls rise
above the Persian carpet's intricate design
of russet islands set in shimmering blues,
while glazed and panelled double doors
reveal a new perspective

where, after breakfast, I've climbed
to a high, hard place, my muscles racked
and sore. Shrunk to the dot of a distant
figure labouring over the tabletop plain,
under the teacup peaks, the eggshell snow,

to the edge, my balance
and sense of proportion waver.
Fear fills my view of the prospect.
The deep blue of repose is so far,
so great the leap into the lap of forgiveness.

# Cherry Blossom

The effect demands a combination of circumstances:
a heavy fall of snow through humid air,
temperature barely below zero
so the snow has a high water content.
Wet and sticky, it thickens boughs
and twigs, lumpy lagging that plugs gaps.

At night the temperature dips,
the snow freezes.

A breeze accompanies the return to zero
in the morning. It clears the sky,
dislodges showers of crystals
and leaves the firmer balls in clumps.

At noon, trees are in full bloom.
Before sunset the horizon pinks,
pinks the snowy branches. Cherry blossom.

# Claire Clairmont And Allegra

It is not true to say that the spirit was crushed
within her by the death of her five-year-old child,
though she said herself she had never again smiled
absolutely; without happiness she could still be happy.

Far from familiar scenes she stepped on strange stairs
to her room's cold and lonely austerity.
But she often remarked, those whom posterity
had honoured with greatness were numbered among her
friends,

though her passage through life had been solitary.
And when she died, in a country remote from her
daughter's grave, the shawl, her lover's last gift to her
sixty years earlier, was laid in the coffin.

When violet evening clouds were edged with orange,
reflected in still water, she watched the day's slow wane.
And though this scene could not remove her pain,
she never tried to believe that her loss negated its beauty.

# A Sunlit Absence

There was a loophole in the day.
Placed right at the outset
and outside
time's measures

it conferred these benefits:
a release for regret,
a way to view
what's happened.

# Transparency

I cannot say it shines, this light,
bruised by the violet flush
of a setting sun on grey rainclouds
that forces its way through a dull pane,

while round my feet I've spread
across the floor a hundred images
or more from the past,
each framed in its square of blue plastic,

each lacking only the right light
to effect a certain kind of release,
the freedom that comes from knowing
that nothing is hidden.

Here they lie, numbered like the years,
like my confusion of the apparent and transparent.

# Giving

Beside this quiet lake in the autumn sun
love sheds its light down transparent years.
The love I thought I'd lost, I've won.

The water's constant ripples make it clear;
the love I thought I'd lost is mine to give.
I'll give it; and giving, the more there is to give.

# Acknowledgements

Acknowledgements are due to the editors of the following magazines and anthologies in which some of these poems first appeared: The Interpreter's House, Links, Carillon, The Reader, Iota, Smiths Knoll, *Saturday Night Desperate* (published by Ragged Raven Press), *Night Balancing* and *Blood Line* (both published by Blinking Eye Publishing). `Tiffany´ won 3rd prize in the 2009 Kent and Sussex poetry competition.

Many of the poems in this collection were workshopped as part of an M.A. in Creative Writing at Manchester Metropolitan University. I would like to express my thanks to my fellow students on the course and to the tutors, Carola Luther and Michael Symmons Roberts, for their valuable comments.

In addition, many poems were also workshopped online at the Just Poets website run by Adele Ward. I am grateful for the many helpful comments and advice that Adele supplied, which played an important part in the evolution of the poems.